MW00826901

Teen Friendship Workbook

Facilitator Reproducible Self-Assessments, Exercises & Educational Handouts

Ester A. Leutenberg
John J. Liptak, EdD

Illustrated by
Amy L. Brodsky, LISW-S

wholeperson
Stress & Wellness Publishers
Duluth, Minnesota

Whole Person
210 West Michigan Street
Duluth, MN 55802-1908

800-247-6789

books@wholeperson.com
www.wholeperson.com

Teen Friendship Workbook
Facilitator Reproducible Self-Assessments,
Exercises & Educational Handouts

Copyright ©2011 by Ester A. Leutenberg and John J. Liptak.
All rights reserved. Except for short excerpts for review purposes
and materials in the assessment, journaling activities, and
educational handouts sections, no part of this book may be
reproduced or transmitted in any form by any means, electronic
or mechanical without permission in writing from the publisher.
Self-assessments, exercises, and educational handouts are meant
to be photocopied.

All efforts have been made to ensure accuracy of the information
contained in this book as of the date published. The author(s)
and the publisher expressly disclaim responsibility for any
adverse effects arising from the use or application of the
information contained herein.

Printed in the United States of America

10 9 8 7 6 5 4 3 2 1

Editorial Director: Carlene Sippola
Art Director: Joy Morgan Dey

Library of Congress Control Number: 2010937661
ISBN: 978-1-57025-249-5

Using This Book *(For the professional)*

Teenagers choosing healthy friendships is of monumental importance! As children enter middle school and high school, they will be experiencing changes in friends, personal style, social life, movies, music, emotions, etc., in fact in all aspects of their lives. They will also meet new friends who are experiencing these same changes. Teens want to spend more time with friends of their own age without supervision. With peers they can feel independent and connected as they develop and experience identities of their own. They will challenge authority, unable to see the value of advice from parents or other adults.

Peer pressure, positive or negative, directs their choices and decisions. The thoughts and actions of peers usually carry more weight than those from parents or other adults. Teenagers may question their family and/or household's rules and values.

Friends can be a positive force for teens. As people mature, they choose friends who share their tastes and values. Good friends influence each other to keep sound values. They will talk each other out of, rather than into, troublesome situations. Positive role modeling in friends affects social behaviors, understanding and acceptance.

Teenagers' social circle may have different thoughts on what's okay and acceptable. Going along with the crowd may be "cool", even though it may involve disobeying parents, not doing schoolwork, risk-taking, and/or keeping up with their friends' material values.

Teenagers who have friends that engage in problem behavior, delinquency, substance abuse, violence, are much more likely to behave the same way. Negative role modeling in friends will influence and encourage poor judgment, bad habits, risky, and possibly illegal behavior. The *Teen Friendship Workbook* will serve as a guide to assist teens in choosing their friends wisely, thus avoiding potentially risky situations. Being able to say "no" and not be negatively influenced by peers is one of the goals of this book.

Choice of friends can make a huge difference. Healthy friendships are full of joy, fun, caring, empathy and mutual support. Friendships grow with time and require a variety of skills that often need to be developed. The goal of this workbook is to help participants explore the skills they are using in their friendships. It incorporates interesting and eye-opening assessments to encourage participants to explore their own personal friendship behavior, as well as that of their friends.

(Continued)

Using This Book (For the professional, continued)

The *Teen Friendship Workbook* contains five separate sections to help teens learn more about themselves and the skills that are fundamental to developing and maintaining healthy friendships. Participating in these exercises will help teens discover and better understand the importance of these skills to live in harmony with a friend or a set of friends.

SECTIONS OF THIS BOOK

Characteristics of Friends Scale

helps teens explore the types of positive and negative qualities their friends possess.

Friendship Skills Scale

helps teens identify the strengths and weakness they possess in interacting with their friends.

Friend Communication Skills Scale

helps teens identify and explore how well they are communicating with their friends and develop better friendship communication skills.

Friendship Personality Scale

helps teens understand their own personality and the personality of their friends to better accept each another for the ways they are different.

Peer Pressure Scale

helps teens identify the ways in which they feel pressured or influenced by their friends to do things they may or may not want to do.

By combining reflective assessment and journaling, participants will be exposed to a powerful method of combining verbalizing and writing to reflect on and solve problems. Participants will become more aware of the strengths and weaknesses of their specific relationship and friendship-building skills.

Preparation for using the assessments and activities in this book is important. The authors suggest that prior to administering any of the assessments in this book, you complete them yourself. (Think back to your teen years.) Working on each assessment yourself will familiarize you with the format of the assessments, the scoring directions, the interpretation guides and the journaling activities. Although the assessments are designed to be self-administered, scored and interpreted, this familiarity will help prepare facilitators to answer questions participants might ask about the assessments.

The Assessments, Journaling Activities and Educational Handouts

The Assessments, Journaling Activities, and Educational Handouts in The *Teen Friendship Workbook* are reproducible and ready to be photocopied for participants' use. Assessments contained in this book focus on self-reported. Accuracy and usefulness of the information provided depends on the truthful information that each participant provides through self-examination. By being honest, participants help themselves to learn about unproductive and ineffective friendship patterns, and to uncover information that might be keeping them from being as happy and/or as successful in friendships as they might be.

Advise the teens using the assessments that they should not spend too much time trying to analyze the content of the questions; their initial response will most likely be true. Regardless of individual scores, encourage participants to write and talk about their findings and their feelings pertaining to what they have discovered about themselves. Exploring teen friendship exercises will be helpful to the teens now and as they mature into adulthood.

Use Codes for Confidentiality

Confidentiality is a term for any action that preserves the privacy of other people. Because the teens completing the activities in this workbook will be asked to answer assessment items and to journal about and explore their relationships with their friends, you will need to discuss confidentiality before you begin using the materials in this workbook. Maintaining confidentiality is important as it shows respect for others and allows the participants to explore their feelings without hurting anyone's feelings or fearing gossip, harm or retribution.

In order to maintain confidentiality, explain to the participants that they need to assign a code name for each person they write about as they complete the various activities in the workbook. For example, a friend named Joey who enjoys going to hockey games might be titled JHG (Joey Hockey Games) for a particular exercise. In order to protect their friends' identities, they may not use people's actual names or initials – just codes.

Thanks to the following whose input in this book has been so valuable!

Teva Belle Kaplan   Lucy Ritzic, OTR/L

Jay Leutenberg   Eileen Regen, M.Ed., CJE

Kathy Liptak, Ed.D.

Layout of the Book

This book includes the following reproducibles in all 5 sections:

- **Assessment Instruments** – Self-assessment inventories with scoring directions and interpretation materials. Group facilitators can choose one or more of the activities relevant to their participants.
- **Activity Handouts** – Practical questions and activities that prompt self-reflection and promote self-understanding. These questions and activities foster introspection and promote pro-social behaviors.
- **Reflective Questions for Journaling** – Self-exploration activities and journaling exercises specific to each assessment to enhance self-discovery, learning, and healing.
- **Educational Handouts** – Handouts designed to supplement instruction can be used individually or in groups. They can be distributed and converted into masters for individual copies, transparencies for overheads, scanned for other digital presentations or written down on a board and discussed.

Who should use this program?

This book has been designed as a practical tool for helping professional therapists, counselors, marriage and family therapists, psychologists, teachers, group leaders, etc. Depending on the role of the professional using The *Teen Friendship Workbook* and the specific group's needs, the sections can be used individually, combined, or implemented as part of an integrated curriculum for a more comprehensive approach.

Why use self-assessments?

Self-assessments are important in teaching various life skills. Participants will . . .

- Become aware of the primary motivators that guide behavior.
- Explore and learn to indentify potentially harmful situations.
- Explore the effects of messages received in childhood.
- Gain insight that will guide behavioral change.
- Focus thinking on behavioral goals for change.
- Uncover resources that can help to cope with problems and difficulties.
- Identify personal characteristics without judgment.
- Develop full awareness of personal strengths and weaknesses.

Because the assessments are presented in a straightforward and easy-to-use format, individuals can self-administer, score, and interpret each assessment independently.

Introduction for the Participant

You and your friends can influence each other in positive and negative ways; your choice of friends is important. By choosing wisely, you and your friends will benefit from your each other. One of the most important aspects in building your friendships is that you always need to be yourself – and true to yourself. You do not need to change who you are, nor should your friends expect you to change for them.

Before you make new friends, or evaluate your present friends, it helps to know what kind of person you want as your friend. It helps to have friends who like to do the same type of things you do and who share the same values that you do. That doesn't mean you have to be exactly like each other, just that you enjoy some of the same things. Sports, books and music are some examples of activities that might be good to have in common. Values might be the importance of family, honesty, good grades, being safe, etc. Without compromising, and sticking to your decisions by being true to yourself, you're bound to find and have friends who are excited about the same things that excite and interest you.

Your friendships may be changing because you and your friends are changing. Teenage years are a time of physical, emotional, and social growth and change. These changes happen at different times, or at different speeds, for each person. You might not need to end old friendships, but these relationships may need to change. You may find that you don't have as much in common with some friends as you used to. It's important to pay attention to your feelings, and to know what you enjoy doing. If your friends seem to be spending more time in actions and activities that you don't enjoy, you might benefit by finding some new friends who share your interests.

Choosing and being a good friend definitely requires a set of skills you can use throughout your life. The *Teen Friendship Workbook* is designed to help you learn more about yourself, identify the effective and ineffective aspects of your friendships, and find better ways to use newfound skills to develop and maintain healthy friendships that bring out the best in you – that help you to be true to yourself.

IMPORTANT

You will be asked to respond to assessment items and to journal about and explore your relationships with your friends. Everyone has the right to confidentiality, and you need to honor the right to privacy of others. Think about it this way – you would not want someone writing things about you that other people could read about. Your friends feel this way also.

In order to maintain the confidentiality of your friends, assign people code names based on things you know about them. For example, a friend named Sherry who loves to wear purple might be coded as SWP (Sherry Wears Purple). Do not use people's actual names when you are listing your friends.

(Continued)

Specific Signs of a Healthy Friendship

- Adaptability
- Pride in each other
- Trust in each other
- Positive peer pressure
- Respect for each other
- Listening to each other
- Shared decision making
- Support in times of need
- Reliability and dependability
- Support of each other's goals
- Caring treatment of each other
- Fun without the need of substances
- Sense of feeling safe with each other
- Acceptance of responsibility for actions
- Encouragement of each other's interests
- Communication is open, honest and direct
- Ease in talking to each other about feelings
- Ability to see from each other's perspective
- Acknowledgement of the need for alone time
- Arguments solved without hurting each other
- Important matters discussed openly and freely
- Laughter and enjoyment of time with each other
- Willingness to listen to and respect the rights of each other
- Apologies sincerely offered when you know you were wrong
- Awareness about how one is treated and how each treats the other
- Encouragement of each other's daily problem-solving and decision-making

Teen Friendship Workbook
TABLE OF CONTENTS

TABLE OF CONTENTS

TABLE OF CONTENTS

TABLE OF CONTENTS

SECTION I:
Characteristics of Friends Scale

Name_____

Date_____

Characteristics of Friends Scale Directions

Friends possess many different characteristics: positive and negative. This scale was designed to help you explore the characteristics your friends have and help you evaluate your relationships.

The Characteristics of Friends Scale contains both positive and negative characteristics. First, list three of your friends on the "friends" lines of the scale. REMEMBER TO USE YOUR CODES FOR YOUR FRIENDS AND NOT THEIR NAMES, for example, Larry likes movies so you will write down **LLM** for *Larry Likes Movies*, rather than Larry. You may list one, two or three friends for the assessment. Next, read each of the statements and decide whether or not the statement describes each friend you have listed. If the statement is like the friend you listed, circle the number next to that item under the "LIKE" column. If the statement is not like the friend you listed, circle the number next to that item under the "NOT LIKE" column. Do not pay attention to the numbers as they will be used for scoring purposes.

In the following example, the person completing the inventory thinks that LLM is a gossip (the circled "Like"), but MPT and ABI are not gossips (the circled numbers under "Not Like").

	Friend #1	**Friend #2**	**Friend #3**
Your friend's code name ⟶	**LLM**	**MPT**	**ABI**
My friend . . .			
	Like Not Like	Like Not Like	Like Not Like
is a gossip	(1) 2	1 (2)	1 (2)

This is not a test and there are no right or wrong answers. Do not spend too much time thinking about your answers. Your initial response will likely be the most true for you.

Be sure to respond to every statement.

(Turn to the next page and begin)

© 2011 WHOLE PERSON ASSOCIATES, 210 WEST MICHIGAN ST., DULUTH MN 55802-1908 • 800-247-6789

Characteristics of Friends Scale

My friend . . .	Friend #1		Friend #2		Friend #3	
Your friend's code name ⟶	_____		_____		_____	
	Like	**Not Like**	**Like**	**Not Like**	**Like**	**Not Like**
is a gossip	1	2	1	2	1	2
is loyal	2	1	2	1	2	1
is honest	2	1	2	1	2	1
tries to pressure me	1	2	1	2	1	2
cares about me	2	1	2	1	2	1
can be trusted	2	1	2	1	2	1
judges me	1	2	1	2	1	2
is reliable	2	1	2	1	2	1
understands me	2	1	2	1	2	1
listens to me	2	1	2	1	2	1
sometimes betrays me	1	2	1	2	1	2
is happy for me	2	1	2	1	2	1
is too competitive	1	2	1	2	1	2
gives me moral support	2	1	2	1	2	1

(Continued on the next page)

© 2011 WHOLE PERSON ASSOCIATES, 210 WEST MICHIGAN ST., DULUTH MN 55802-1908 ▪ 800-247-6789

(Characteristics of Friends Scale continued)

My friend . . .	Friend #1 Like	Friend #1 Not Like	Friend #2 Like	Friend #2 Not Like	Friend #3 Like	Friend #3 Not Like
is self-centered	1	2	1	2	1	2
is manipulative	1	2	1	2	1	2
is trustworthy	2	1	2	1	2	1
is jealous of me	1	2	1	2	1	2
is open-minded	2	1	2	1	2	1
treats me badly sometimes	1	2	1	2	1	2
is helpful	2	1	2	1	2	1
is forgiving	2	1	2	1	2	1
is a bully	1	2	1	2	1	2
is a snob	1	2	1	2	1	2
is always there for me	2	1	2	1	2	1

Your friend's code name ⟶ _____

Total #1 _____ **Total #2** _____ **Total #3** _____

(Go to the Scoring Directions on the next page)

© 2011 WHOLE PERSON ASSOCIATES, 210 WEST MICHIGAN ST., DULUTH MN 55802-1908 • 800-247-6789

Characteristics of Friends Scale
Scoring Directions

This scale is designed to identify both the positive and negative characteristics of your friends. To get your scores for each of the friends you listed, total all the circled numbers from both columns for each friend. You will get a number from 25 to 50 for each friend. Put that number at the end of each column. Then, transfer your scores to the lines below.

Friend #1 – code _____   **TOTAL**   **=**   _____

Friend #2 – code _____   **TOTAL**   **=**   _____

Friend #3 – code _____   **TOTAL**   **=**   _____

Profile Interpretation

Total Scale Scores	Result	Indications
42 to 50	high	Scores in this category indicates **many** of the characteristics of a true friend. They are loyal, trustworthy, want to see you succeed, and will be there for you when you need them.
34 to 41	moderate	Scores in this category indicates **some** of the characteristics of a true friend.
25 to 33	low	Scores in this category indicates **few** of the characteristics of a true friend.

The exercises that follow will help you to explore your relationship with your friends. Complete all of the activities and exercises to help you choose your friends wisely and to be a true friend.

© 2011 WHOLE PERSON ASSOCIATES, 210 WEST MICHIGAN ST., DULUTH MN 55802-1908 • 800-247-6789

My Friends

Your friends probably fall into several categories. You probably have people who are: acquaintances (you know them to say hello, but you do not hang out with them socially), friends (people you know and may hang out with, but you may not share personal secrets), and true friends. When responding to the questions, use your friends' codes.

Who are your acquaintances?

_____

_____

_____

_____

_____

Who are your friends?

_____

_____

_____

_____

_____

Who are your true friends?

_____

_____

_____

_____

_____

_____

(Continued on the next page)

© 2011 WHOLE PERSON ASSOCIATES, 210 WEST MICHIGAN ST., DULUTH MN 55802-1908 ▪ 800-247-6789

My Friends *(Continued)*

What are the current trends among your peers (dress, food, things to do, etc.)?

_____

_____

_____

_____

_____

Which of these trends do you follow?

_____

_____

_____

_____

_____

List the codes of your friends. Where do you like to go with each one?

_____

_____

_____

_____

_____

List the codes of your friends. What you like to do with each one?

_____

_____

_____

_____

_____

(Continued on the next page)

My Friends *(Continued)*

What do you **not** like to do that your friends do like to do?

_____

_____

_____

_____

_____

What do you like to do that your friends do **not** like to do?

_____

_____

_____

_____

_____

_____

How would you define a *True Friendship*?

_____

_____

_____

_____

_____

_____

List the codes of the friends that you consider to be *True Friends*.

_____   _____   _____   _____   _____

_____   _____   _____   _____   _____

_____   _____   _____   _____   _____

My Friends' Characteristics

Think about your friends. Below, list the codes of your friends and then their positive characteristics and their negative characteristics. You may list the friends from the assessment, or other friends you have. Be as specific as possible.

MY FRIENDS (code)	POSITIVE CHARACTERISTICS	NEGATIVE CHARACTERISTICS

© 2011 WHOLE PERSON ASSOCIATES, 210 WEST MICHIGAN ST., DULUTH MN 55802-1908 ▪ 800-247-6789

SECTION I: ACTIVITY HANDOUTS

Being a Better Friend

Everyone can improve their friendship skills. Think about the friendships you have and list some of the things you could do to be a better friend.

FRIENDSHIP SKILLS	WHAT I WILL DO
Be reliable	
Spend more time	
Be empathetic	
Be supportive	
Be willing to compromise	
Disagree respectfully	
Listen	

(Continued on the next page)

© 2011 WHOLE PERSON ASSOCIATES, 210 WEST MICHIGAN ST., DULUTH MN 55802-1908 • 800-247-6789

23

Being a Better Friend (Continued)

FRIENDSHIP SKILLS	WHAT I WILL DO
Respect choices	
Encourage dreams	
Keep confidences unless dangerous or risky	
Share thoughts and concerns	
Not be overly possessive or jealous	
Want what's best for my friend	
Be truthful	
Other _____	

© 2011 WHOLE PERSON ASSOCIATES, 210 WEST MICHIGAN ST., DULUTH MN 55802-1908 ▪ 800-247-6789

Friends Helping Friends

In the spaces, answer the following questions about your true friends and good friends. Write their code and your response.

My friends show how much they care for me when . . .

(Ex. CRH – she calls to see if I'm OK when I don't come to school one day.)

_____

_____

_____

My friends support me when . . .

_____

_____

_____

My friends have helped me to . . .

_____

_____

_____

My friends influence me positively by . . .

_____

_____

_____

I can lean on my friends for things like . . .

_____

_____

_____

My friends appreciate it when I . . .

_____

_____

_____

Toxic Friends

Some friends have a toxic effect on their peers. In the spaces, answer the following questions about your true friends and good friends. Write their code and your response.

My friends use me for other purposes . . .

(Ex. CRH – he only includes me when he needs a ride.)

_____

_____

_____

My friends try to control me by . . .

_____

_____

_____

My friends are critical of me when I . . .

_____

_____

_____

My friends break promises about . . .

_____

_____

_____

My friends gossip a lot about . . .

_____

_____

_____

My friends compete with me about . . .

_____

_____

_____

© 2011 WHOLE PERSON ASSOCIATES, 210 WEST MICHIGAN ST., DULUTH MN 55802-1908 ▪ 800-247-6789

Types of Friendships

In the past, friends were people with whom you would spend time. Now, many people have friends they may never meet face-to-face. Your friends may be people with whom you hang out, or they may be people you meet on social networking sites, over the Internet, text or just talking to on the telephone. Write about the friends (using their code name) you have in each of the various formats.

1) Friends you see a lot of the time

Who are these friends and when and where do you see them?

(Ex. CRH – We go back and forth to school every day.)

_____

_____

_____

_____

_____

_____

_____

_____

2) Cell phone friends

Who are these friends (using their codes) and how many hours a day to you spend talking with them on your cell phone? What do you talk about?

(Ex. LLR – We talk about an hour every night. We do homework together.)

_____

_____

_____

_____

_____

_____

_____

(Continued on the next page)

TYPES OF FRIENDSHIPS *(Continued)*

3) Texting

Do you have friends that you primarily text? Where are you when you text? Are you safe?
(Ex. LOL – We talk all day long. I'm probably not so safe when I'm walking, not looking.)

_____

_____

_____

_____

_____

4) Email and Chat Rooms

What chat rooms do you and your friends use? How much time do you spend each day with friends on the computer? How do you decide what is a reasonable amount of time to spend?
(Ex. TMF – Probably 2 hours a day. Too much when I have a lot of homework.)

_____

_____

_____

_____

_____

5) Social Networking Sites (Facebook, Twitter, etc.)

Do you use social networking sites? How do you react when you think they become too personal?
(Ex. I find out some personal things about people I hardly know.)

_____

_____

_____

_____

_____

© 2011 WHOLE PERSON ASSOCIATES, 210 WEST MICHIGAN ST., DULUTH MN 55802-1908 ▪ 800-247-6789

Ex-Friends

Many friendships don't last forever, nor may you want them to. Friendships may end for different reasons and under different circumstances. In the table that follows, think about past friendships that ended. In the left-hand column, list the code of your ex-friends and in the right-hand column list the reason for the separation (grew apart, argument, death, moved away, went to college, etc.).

Ex-Friends	Why are they an Ex-Friend	Could that friendship been saved?
Ex. NAM	We had an argument and we were too angry to try to resolve it.	Maybe if we tried after we calmed down.

Quotations ~ Friendship

Place check marks by the quotes that you feel would inspire you to evaluate your friendships. You can cut the quote out and post it by your computer or on your refrigerator or tuck it in your wallet. You can give or send it to a friend or an ex-friend. At the bottom of the page, write why those particular quotes speak to you.

A friend is a gift you can give to yourself. ~ **Robert Louis Stevenson**

If you judge people, you have no time to love them. ~ **Mother Teresa**

You never lose by loving. You always lose by holding back. ~ **Barbara DeAngelis**

Every gift from a friend is a wish for your happiness. ~ **Richard Bach**

Remember, the greatest gift is not found in a store nor under a tree, but in the hearts of true friends. ~ **Andy Lew**

Friends are the bacon bits in the salad of life. ~ **Anon**

I selected the quotation(s) above because . . .

_____

_____

_____

_____

_____

_____

_____

_____

_____

_____

_____

   © 2011 WHOLE PERSON ASSOCIATES, 210 WEST MICHIGAN ST., DULUTH MN 55802-1908 ▪ 800-247-6789

My Friends and I

My favorite friendship story is . . .

_____

_____

_____

_____

_____

_____

_____

_____

_____

_____

_____

My least favorite friendship story is . . .

_____

_____

_____

_____

_____

_____

_____

_____

_____

_____

_____

_____

Assertiveness

Communication styles:

- Passive
- Assertive
- Aggressive
- Passive-Aggressive

Ideally, being assertive is the way to go! It is direct and honest communication of your feelings, opinions, needs and rights in a way that doesn't violate the personal rights of others. These tips might help you to be more assertive.

- Use an even, calm voice – even when angry
- Say no – without feeling guilty
- Set your own priorities
- Decide how you want to spend your time
- Ask for what you want
- Be clear and to the point
- Use I statements
- Accept helpful criticism
- Do not judge or name call

 © 2011 WHOLE PERSON ASSOCIATES, 210 WEST MICHIGAN ST., DULUTH MN 55802-1908 ▪ 800-247-6789

Shyness

Many teens say that it is difficult to make friends because they are so shy.

Here are some tips to help you overcome your shyness:

- Accept your shyness as something to work on.

- Imagine you are enjoying yourself – you might!

- Find your strengths and focus on using them.

- Be friendly, stand tall, use eye contact.

- Use positive affirmations like "I am shy, but I won't let that stop me."

- Ask questions. People like to talk about themselves.

- If you have an idea that deserves to be heard – speak up!

- Warm up to the challenge of approaching people who might become friends.

- Take a breath and introduce yourself.

- Rehearse a sentence that you can say to a new person to introduce yourself.

- Journal your successes.

- Remember – you are special!

© 2011 WHOLE PERSON ASSOCIATES, 210 WEST MICHIGAN ST., DULUTH MN 55802-1908 ▪ 800-247-6789

© 2011 WHOLE PERSON ASSOCIATES, 210 WEST MICHIGAN ST., DULUTH MN 55802-1908 ▪ 800-247-6789

SECTION II:
Friendship Skills Scale

Name_____

Date_____

© 2011 WHOLE PERSON ASSOCIATES, 210 WEST MICHIGAN ST., DULUTH MN 55802-1908 • 800-247-6789

Friendship Skills Scale Directions

You probably have many different types of friends. To be a good friend you need a variety of skills. Some of these skills may come easily to you, while others do not and you may need to work on them. The Friendship Skills Scale can help you identify and explore the skills you use while interacting with your friends.

This assessment contains 42 statements. Use the choices listed below to respond to the statement. You can complete the items based on one specific friendship or on many different friendships. Read each of the statements and circle the number to the right that best describes how much you value each statement. In the statement below, the **circled 2** means that the statement is a little like the test taker.

Circle **1** if the statement is **Not at All Like Me**   Circle **3** if the statement is **Quite a Bit Like Me**

Circle **2** if the statement is **A Little Bit Like Me**   Circle **4** if the statement is **A Lot Like Me**

With my friends . . .

I am honest   1 (2) 3 4

This is not a test and there are no right or wrong answers. Do not spend too much time thinking about your answers. Your initial response will likely be the most true for you. Be sure to respond to every statement.

(Turn to the next page and begin)

© 2011 WHOLE PERSON ASSOCIATES, 210 WEST MICHIGAN ST., DULUTH MN 55802-1908 ▪ 800-247-6789

Friendship Skills Scale

Circle **1** if the statement is **Not at All Like Me**   Circle **3** if the statement is **Quite a Bit Like Me**

Circle **2** if the statement is **A Little Bit Like Me**   Circle **4** if the statement is **A Lot Like Me**

With my friends . . .

I am honest	1	2	3	4
I feel like I am assertive	1	2	3	4
I stick with them in good and bad times	1	2	3	4
I think they can trust me	1	2	3	4
I do not gossip about them	1	2	3	4
I am dependable	1	2	3	4
I do not do anything to damage their reputations	1	2	3	4

H TOTAL = _____

With my friends . . .

I do not drag them into situations that make them uncomfortable	1	2	3	4
I am supportive of the things they do	1	2	3	4
I am loyal to them	1	2	3	4
I am not jealous of their success	1	2	3	4
I am there in hard times	1	2	3	4
I am not reluctant to stick up for them	1	2	3	4
I do not try to convince them to do things my way	1	2	3	4

S TOTAL = _____

(Continued on the next page)

© 2011 WHOLE PERSON ASSOCIATES, 210 WEST MICHIGAN ST., DULUTH MN 55802-1908 ▪ 800-247-6789

(Friendship Skills Scale continued)

Circle **1** if the statement is **Not at All Like Me**   Circle **3** if the statement is **Quite a Bit Like Me**
Circle **2** if the statement is **A Little Bit Like Me**   Circle **4** if the statement is **A Lot Like Me**

With my friends . . .

I accept them for who they are	1	2	3	4
I do not judge them if they are different	1	2	3	4
I do not stereotype them	1	2	3	4
I respect the differences in the money we can spend	1	2	3	4
I treat everyone the same, regardless of cultural or ethnic background	1	2	3	4
I try to learn from them	1	2	3	4
I do not need my friends to be just like me	1	2	3	4

T TOTAL = _____

With my friends . . .

I show concern for them	1	2	3	4
I understand them and their feelings	1	2	3	4
I am forgiving	1	2	3	4
I like them regardless of what they own or how they live	1	2	3	4
I listen when they have concerns	1	2	3	4
I am generous with them	1	2	3	4
I am not mean, cruel or insensitive	1	2	3	4

C TOTAL = _____

(Continued on the next page)

© 2011 WHOLE PERSON ASSOCIATES, 210 WEST MICHIGAN ST., DULUTH MN 55802-1908 ▪ 800-247-6789

(Friendship Skills Scale continued)

Circle **1** if the statement is **Not at All Like Me**   Circle **3** if the statement is **Quite a Bit Like Me**

Circle **2** if the statement is **A Little Bit Like Me**   Circle **4** if the statement is **A Lot Like Me**

With my friends . . .

I respect their beliefs	1	2	3	4
I try to understand their problems	1	2	3	4
I take them seriously	1	2	3	4
I do not make fun or tease them	1	2	3	4
I encourage them to become all they can be	1	2	3	4
I feel good when they do well	1	2	3	4
I draw the line when they want me to do things I don't want to do	1	2	3	4

R TOTAL = _____

With my friends . . .

I am thankful for who they are	1	2	3	4
I feel appreciated for who I am	1	2	3	4
I do not try to change who I am to please them	1	2	3	4
I feel comfortable around them	1	2	3	4
I show them how much I appreciate them	1	2	3	4
I express my thanks to them	1	2	3	4
I am grateful for what they add to my life	1	2	3	4

A TOTAL = _____

(Go to the Scoring Directions on the next page)

© 2011 WHOLE PERSON ASSOCIATES, 210 WEST MICHIGAN ST., DULUTH MN 55802-1908 ▪ 800-247-6789

Friendship Skills Scale
Scoring Directions

Beginning and maintaining friendships is not always easy and having friendship skills is helpful. The Friendship Skills Scale is designed to measure the specific skills you are currently using in your friendships and then help you to develop additional skills to help you to be an even more effective friend.

For each of the sections you completed, add the numbers you circled in the column for each section. Put that total on the line marked TOTAL at the end of the section.

Then add them together to find your Overall Friendship Skills Grand Total.

Then, transfer your totals to the spaces below:

H = **HONEST & TRUSTWORTHY**   **TOTAL**   =   _____

S = **SUPPORTIVE**   **TOTAL**   =   _____

T = **TOLERANT**   **TOTAL**   =   _____

C = **CARING**   **TOTAL**   =   _____

R = **RESPECTFUL**   **TOTAL**   =   _____

A = **APPRECIATIVE**   **TOTAL**   =   _____

OVERALL FRIENDSHIP GRAND TOTAL   =   _____

Profile Interpretation

Individual Skill Scale Score	Overall Friendship Scale Score	Result	Indications
7 to 13	**42 to 79**	low	You could probably benefit from using friendship skills to allow you to be a better friend. The exercises and activities that follow will help you.
14 to 21	**84 to 126**	moderate	You probably possess some friendship skills that allow you to be a good friend. The exercises and activities that follow will help you develop more.
22 to 28	**126 to 168**	high	You seem to have friendship skills to be a very good friend. The exercises and activities that follow can help you sharpen those skills.

Friendship Skills Scale Descriptions

Honest & Trustworthy

People scoring high on this scale try to be clear about their intentions and are honest with their friends. They try to present a clear picture of who they are and show that they can be trusted not to gossip about their friends.

Supportive

People scoring high on this scale are supportive of their friends, both in good times and bad. They will stick by their friends and be loyal and helpful when situations are tough.

Tolerant

People scoring high on this scale are accepting of such differences as culture, race, socio-economic status, and religion. They not only accept differences in people, but they look at these differences as an opportunity to learn and experience new things.

Caring

People scoring high on this scale genuinely care about their friends. They like them or who they are and listen to them when the need arises. They are able to keep friends and will never tease them or treat them unkindly or cruelly.

Respectful

People scoring high on this scale respect their friends for the way they live their lives and for what they have to offer. They enjoy times when their friends do well and support them.

Appreciative

People scoring high on this scale truly appreciate their friends for who they are as individuals. They feel comfortable around them and are thankful for them. They are not afraid to show and tell their friends how much they are appreciated.

The higher the total number for each section, the more you tend to use those skills with your friends. No matter whether you scored **Low**, **Moderate** or **High**, the exercises and activities that follow are designed to help you explore your basic friendship skills.

 © 2011 WHOLE PERSON ASSOCIATES, 210 WEST MICHIGAN ST., DULUTH MN 55802-1908 ▪ 800-247-6789

Honest & Trustworthy

How do you know when you can trust people?

_____
_____
_____
_____

Who is a friend you can trust? (use a code) Why do you trust this friend?

_____
_____
_____
_____

How important is trust to you? Why?

_____
_____
_____
_____

How do you feel when people are dishonest with you?

_____
_____
_____
_____

In what ways are you not honest with your friends? Describe one or two situations.

_____
_____
_____
_____

Supportive

Describe how you and your friends support each other.

_____

_____

_____

_____

How important is support in your friendships?

_____

_____

_____

_____

How do you/would you feel when your friends fail to stick up for you?

_____

_____

_____

_____

How have you been unsupportive to friends?

_____

_____

_____

_____

How can you "be there" more for your friends?

_____

_____

_____

_____

© 2011 WHOLE PERSON ASSOCIATES, 210 WEST MICHIGAN ST., DULUTH MN 55802-1908 ▪ 800-247-6789

Tolerant

What types of things are you open-minded about (gender, culture, etc.)?

_____

_____

_____

_____

In general, how would you say that you treat your friends?

_____

_____

_____

_____

How do you like to be treated?

_____

_____

_____

_____

What things will you not tolerate from your friends?

_____

_____

_____

_____

How do you react to friends who are not fair to you?

_____

_____

_____

_____

Caring

How do you and your friends show that you care for each other?

_____

_____

_____

What does caring have to do with friendship in general?

_____

_____

_____

In what ways are you mean or insensitive to your friends?

_____

_____

_____

How do your friends show a lack of caring about you?

_____

_____

_____

How are you charitable to your friends?

_____

_____

_____

How do you show that you care about your friends' needs and problems?

_____

_____

_____

© 2011 WHOLE PERSON ASSOCIATES, 210 WEST MICHIGAN ST., DULUTH MN 55802-1908 • 800-247-6789

Respectful

How are put-downs a sign of disrespect?

_____

_____

_____

How do/can you respect people who are different from you?

_____

_____

_____

What is a recent time when you treated a friend (use code) respectfully?

_____

_____

_____

Describe a time when you felt disrespected by a friend (use code). How did you feel?

_____

_____

_____

What is a common sign of disrespect with the friends you know?

_____

_____

_____

In what ways have you been disrespected? How have you disrespected others?

_____

_____

_____

© 2011 WHOLE PERSON ASSOCIATES, 210 WEST MICHIGAN ST., DULUTH MN 55802-1908 • 800-247-6789

Appreciative

What do your friends add to your life?

_____

_____

_____

What do you add to the lives of your friends?

_____

_____

_____

How do you show your friends your appreciation?

_____

_____

_____

How do your friends show you that they appreciate you?

_____

_____

_____

How do you feel when you are not appreciated?

_____

_____

_____

For which friends are you most thankful? (use codes) Why?

_____

_____

_____

 © 2011 WHOLE PERSON ASSOCIATES, 210 WEST MICHIGAN ST., DULUTH MN 55802-1908 ▪ 800-247-6789

Showing Friendship

Use your newfound friendship skills to be a better friend.

In the right-hand column list the ways you will be a better friend to others.

FRIENDSHIP SKILLS	HOW I WILL BE A BETTER FRIEND
Honest & Trustworthy	
Supportive	
Tolerant	
Caring	
Respectful	
Appreciative	

© 2011 WHOLE PERSON ASSOCIATES, 210 WEST MICHIGAN ST., DULUTH MN 55802-1908 ▪ 800-247-6789

My Friends

In the spaces that follow, examine the relationships you have with your various friends. List one friend's code in each of the three sections and then describe how he or she shows you the various critical skills required of a friend.

Friend's code name: _____

Honest & Trustworthy	
Supportive	
Tolerant	
Caring	
Respectful	
Appreciative	

Friend's code name: _____

Honest & Trustworthy	
Supportive	
Tolerant	
Caring	
Respectful	
Appreciative	

© 2011 WHOLE PERSON ASSOCIATES, 210 WEST MICHIGAN ST., DULUTH MN 55802-1908 ▪ 800-247-6789

My Friends (Continued)

Friend's code name: _____

Honest & Trustworthy	
Supportive	
Tolerant	
Caring	
Respectful	
Appreciative	

What did you learn about your friends from this exercise?

_____

_____

_____

How has this changed the way you feel about your friends?

_____

_____

_____

In what ways have these skills changed as you and your friends have become more mature?

_____

_____

_____

© 2011 WHOLE PERSON ASSOCIATES, 210 WEST MICHIGAN ST., DULUTH MN 55802-1908 ▪ 800-247-6789

Friendship Quotations

Choose two of the quotes below. How does each speak to your friendships?
Perhaps you will find a quote that you disagree with. Write about that also.

I can trust my friends. These people force me to examine, encourage me to grow. ~ **Cher**

A real friend is one who walks in when the rest of the world walks out. ~ **Walter Winchell**

A friend is one who knows us, but loves us anyway. ~ **Fr. Jerome Cummings**

_____

_____

_____

_____

_____

_____

_____

_____

_____

_____

_____

_____

_____

_____

_____

_____

_____

_____

© 2011 WHOLE PERSON ASSOCIATES, 210 WEST MICHIGAN ST., DULUTH MN 55802-1908 ▪ 800-247-6789

Qualities in a Friendship

What qualities do you look for in a friend?

_____

_____

_____

_____

_____

_____

_____

_____

How can you tell the difference between sincere and insincere friends?

_____

_____

_____

_____

_____

_____

_____

_____

How can you start being a better friend to others?

_____

_____

_____

_____

_____

_____

_____

_____

© 2011 WHOLE PERSON ASSOCIATES, 210 WEST MICHIGAN ST., DULUTH MN 55802-1908 ▪ 800-247-6789

How to Make Friends

- Look at everyone as a potential friend
- Be friendly
- Make the first move
- Smile
- Be picky
- Ask questions and listen
- Be yourself
- Look past differences in people
- Be authentic
- Keep trying
- Relax and exhibit confidence
- Overcome shyness
- Join community-sponsored groups
- Get involved in school activities
- Volunteer with worthwhile clubs and organizations

Remember to be safe in interacting with people you do not know.

   © 2011 WHOLE PERSON ASSOCIATES, 210 WEST MICHIGAN ST., DULUTH MN 55802-1908 • 800-247-6789

Where You Can Find Friends

- School

- Neighborhood

- Afterschool-sponsored groups

- Sports

- Family friends

- Clubs and organizations

- Places of Worship

- Work

- Hobby group activities

- Virtual Activities

Remember to be safe in interacting with people you do not know.

© 2011 WHOLE PERSON ASSOCIATES, 210 WEST MICHIGAN ST., DULUTH MN 55802-1908 ▪ 800-247-6789

SECTION III:
Friend Communication Skills Scale

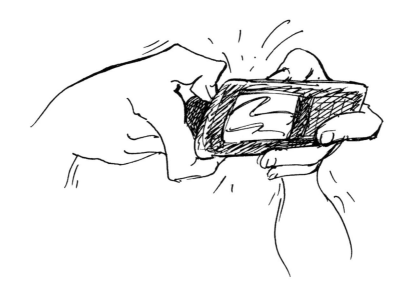

Name_____

Date_____

© 2011 WHOLE PERSON ASSOCIATES, 210 WEST MICHIGAN ST., DULUTH MN 55802-1908 ▪ 800-247-6789

Friend Communication Skills Scale Directions

Communication is the exchange of thoughts, opinions and information with your friends. It is the way you relate to them on an interpersonal level. Communication involves talking and listening to your friends, asserting yourself when you need to and arguing appropriately. Whether you are sharing personal experiences or talking about what each of you would like to do on the weekend, you are using communication skills. Open, honest and direct communication is critical in any healthy friendship.

The Friend Communications Skills Scale can help you explore how well you are communicating with your friends. Choose one of your friends whom you will be thinking of as you complete the assessment. It contains 50 statements. Read each of the statements and decide how much you agree. T represents true and F represents false.

In the following example, the circled **F** indicates that the statement is FALSE for the person completing the scale:

When I am talking with my friend, I . . .

1. use language my friend can understand   T   Ⓕ

This is not a test and there are no right or wrong answers. Do not spend too much time thinking about your answers. Your initial response will likely be the most true for you. Be sure to respond to every statement.

At this point, think about one of your friends as you answer the questions on the assessment that follows.

(Turn to the next page and begin)

© 2011 WHOLE PERSON ASSOCIATES, 210 WEST MICHIGAN ST., DULUTH MN 55802-1908 ▪ 800-247-6789

Friend Communication Skills Scale

Friend's code name: _____

When I am talking with this friend, I . . .

1. use language my friend can understand	T	F
2. usually understand what my friend is saying	T	F
3. will clarify my friend's statement if I don't understand something	T	F
4. am straightforward and direct	T	F
5. say what I feel so that my friend does not have to read my mind	T	F
6. check to make sure my friend hears and understands what I say	T	F
7. use "I" statements to take responsibility for what I am saying	T	F
8. ask for feedback about what I say	T	F
9. make sure my friend understands my body language	T	F
10. talk for myself, and rarely say "everybody..." or "they say..."	T	F

DM – TOTAL T's = _____

When this friend and I disagree about something, I . . .

11. usually blame my friend	T	F
12. make threats like "I won't be your friend anymore if..."	T	F
13. call my friend names	T	F
14. rarely take responsibility for my part	T	F
15. bring up past disagreements	T	F
16. often speak and act in ways that make my friend feel bad	T	F
17. tease and mock my friend	T	F
18. raise my voice, even though I may not be aware of it at the time	T	F
19. send negative messages such as "you're fat, stupid, _____."	T	F
20. try and defend my position, even if I know I am wrong	T	F

DA – TOTAL F's = _____

(Continued on the next page)

© 2011 WHOLE PERSON ASSOCIATES, 210 WEST MICHIGAN ST., DULUTH MN 55802-1908 ▪ 800-247-6789

(Friend Communication Skills Scale continued)

When this friend asks too much of me, I . . .

21. think it is selfish to put my needs before my friend's needs		T	F
22. fear that my friend will get angry if I disagree		T	F
23. have a hard time standing up for myself		T	F
24. wish I could ask for what I want more often		T	F
25. am too passive and I regret it later		T	F
26. will not express my opinion if it is different		T	F
27. do not like to make my friend angry, so I go along		T	F
28. rarely question my friend		T	F
29. hesitate to tell my friend how I feel		T	F
30. always try to accommodate my friend		T	F

BA – TOTAL F's = _____

When I listen to this friend, I . . .

31. am good at reading non-verbal cues and body language		T	F
32. usually hear and pay attention		T	F
33. do not interrupt		T	F
34. ask for explanations if I do not understand something said		T	F
35. notice the feelings behind what my friend is saying		T	F
36. am careful to show positive body language		T	F
37. allow my friend enough time to express a viewpoint		T	F
38. try not to get defensive		T	F
39. attempt to remain optimistic		T	F
40. am sure to look at the situation from my friend's point of view		T	F

AL – TOTAL T's = _____

When this friend and I argue, I . . .

41. usually respond to anger by getting angry at myself		T	F
42. sometimes say things that are insulting		T	F
43. tease more than I should		T	F
44. complain about my friend to others		T	F
45. get angry and shout		T	F
46. frequently bring up past mistakes		T	F
47. say cruel remarks		T	F
48. make personal attacks		T	F
49. lose control once I get started		T	F
50. criticize too harshly		T	F

CF – TOTAL F's = _____

(Go to the Scoring Directions on the next page)

© 2011 WHOLE PERSON ASSOCIATES, 210 WEST MICHIGAN ST., DULUTH MN 55802-1908 ▪ 800-247-6789

Friend Communication Skills Scale Scoring

The Friend Communication Skills Scale is designed to measure how well you are able to communicate with your friends. Five important aspects of communicating effectively include sending direct messages, having controlled arguments, being assertive when you need to be, listening actively to what your friends say, and criticizing and arguing fairly. These make up the five scales on the assessment.

Scoring the assessment is a very easy process. Look at the questions you just answered.

- For Items **1-10**, count the number of T answers you circled. Put this score on the **DM-TOTAL**. (Direct Messages)

- For Items **11-20**, count the number of F answers you circled. Put this score on the **DA-TOTAL**. (Disagreeing and Arguing)

- For Items **21-30**, count the number of F answers you circled. Put this score on the **BA-TOTAL**. (Being Assertive)

- For Items **31-40**, count the number of T answers you circled. Put this score on the **AL-TOTAL**. (Actively Listening)

- For Items **41-50**, count the number of F answers you circled. Put this score on the **CF-TOTAL**. (Criticizing and Fighting)

Now, transfer your totals to the spaces below:

DM – Direct Messages = _____

DA – Disagreeing and Arguing = _____

BA – Being Assertive = _____

AL – Actively Listening = _____

CF – Criticizing and Fighting = _____

TOTAL COMMUNICATION SKILLS SCORE _____

What patterns do you notice?

_____

_____

How will these results help you in your relationships with your friends?

_____

_____

What are the most important areas you need to work on?

_____

_____

© 2011 WHOLE PERSON ASSOCIATES, 210 WEST MICHIGAN ST., DULUTH MN 55802-1908 ▪ 800-247-6789

Friend Communication Scale
Profile Interpretation

Communication is important in good relationships. When you improve how you communicate with your friends, you will begin to notice closer relationships, deeper understanding of each other's thoughts and feelings, and fewer disagreements. This assessment will help you explore how effective you are in five critical components of effective communication, as well as your overall communications skills. Look at the profile interpretation materials below.

Total Individual Scale Scores	Total Communication Skills Scale Score	Result	Indications
7 to 10	34 to 50	high	You are able to communicate well with your friends a great deal of the time. Continue to use these effective communication skills when interacting with your friends. You will enjoy completing the exercises in this chapter.
4 to 6	17 to 33	moderate	Most of the time, you are able to communicate well with your friends. Continue to use the communication skills you are already using when interacting with your friends, and complete the exercises contained in this chapter for even more effective communication.
0 to 3	0 to 16	low	You are probably not often able to communicate well with your friends. Complete the exercises contained in this chapter to assist you in discovering more effective communication skills you can use with your friends.

Regardless of your score on the assessment, all of the following exercises have been designed to help you increase your communication skills.

Messages

Most arguments among friends are the result of sending poor messages to one another. For example, a friend who misunderstands something you say can be offended and get angry with you. To communicate effectively with your friends, it is necessary that your friends understand what you are saying and that you truly understand what they are saying. To be more effective in communicating with your friends, consider these guidelines to make certain your messages are heard and understood by your friends:

- **When you talk with your friends, take responsibility for what you say.** Use words like I, me and my, to communicate your message. In this way you "own" the messages you send to them. Take responsibility for your own words. When you use words like "they said" or "some people," you put the responsibility of what you are saying onto someone else. Using "you" often sounds threatening, aggressive and blaming, whereas creating I-messages conveys your comments is a positive way.

- **Maintain eye contact and speak directly to your friends.**

- **When asking questions, avoid questions that require a yes-no answer.** (Did you and RSN go to the movies?) Instead, use questions that allow your friend the chance to tell you what happened. (What did you and RSN do yesterday?)

- **Express your feelings using I statements when talking with your friends.** (I feel angry when you don't ask Janie to go with us!) or (I get angry when you don't ever want to come over to my house.)

In the boxes on the left-hand side of the table, list the situations that frustrate you with your friends. In the right-hand column, express your feelings to that person, using the guidelines you just read about.

Now You Try

Situations That Frustrate Me (use code name)	What I Would Like to Say to My Friends
Ex: GWA drives too fast.	Ex: GWA, when you drive fast I am afraid that we are going to be in an accident.

© 2011 WHOLE PERSON ASSOCIATES, 210 WEST MICHIGAN ST., DULUTH MN 55802-1908 ▪ 800-247-6789

Disagreeing and Arguing

Effective listening and communicating will certainly improve the relationships you have with your friends. However, you should remember that conflicts and disagreements are part of any friendship. These disagreements will arise for a variety of reasons including differences in opinions, misunderstandings, opposing ideas, unrealistic expectations, and mistreatment to name a few. When you find yourself beginning to argue with one of your friends, try to understand what is really happening and what you and your friend are really arguing about.

In the left-hand column of the table that follows, list the things that trigger most of the arguments between you and your friends. Then, in the right-hand column, try to get to the bottom of the issues and see what is really triggering most of your fights. Use code.

Triggers for Arguments (use code name)	**What We Are Really Arguing About**
Ex: MRG asks me to go me to parties where there is drinking. I don't want to go, but I'm afraid of losing her friendship.	Ex: Only I know what's best for me, and I don't want people making decisions for me or pressuring me into doing things I don't want to do.

Assertiveness

Assertiveness is asking for what you need in an honest, open and direct way. Assertive people are able to express their feelings, thoughts, desires, needs and wants, calmly and directly. This takes practice. Use codes.

Why is it so difficult to ask your friends what you need and want?

_____

_____

_____

What typically happens when you do?

_____

_____

_____

My Complaints

About My Friends (use code name)	**How My Friends Can Make Me Happier**
Ex: JDB is standoffish when it comes to letting others into our circle of friends	Ex: She can welcome diverse people into our circle of friends

© 2011 WHOLE PERSON ASSOCIATES, 210 WEST MICHIGAN ST., DULUTH MN 55802-1908 ▪ 800-247-6789

What I Want and Do Not Want from My Friends

To be assertive, you must know what you want and do not want from your friends and from your relationships with them. By establishing what it is that you really want, you will be able to ask for what you want and need without being afraid of their getting angry at you. You will be able to make decisions for yourself about what types of things you need.

In the boxes on the right, list what you want and do not want from your friends in each of the categories.

CATEGORIES	WHAT I WANT FROM MY FRIENDS (use code name)	WHAT I DO NOT WANT FROM MY FRIENDS
Ex: Support	Ex: I want JRS to be more understanding of the amount of time I need to babysit.	Ex: I don't want HLN to kid me about joining a Political Club at school.
Support		
Bullying		
Peer Pressure		
Respect of Parents		
Honesty and Trust		
Popularity/Status		
Intimacy		
Dress/Hygiene		
Electronic Communication		
Community Involvement		
Interests		
Verbal Communication		

(Continued on the next page)

What I Want and Do Not Want from My Friends *(Continued)*

CATEGORIES	WHAT I WANT FROM MY FRIENDS (use code name)	WHAT I DO NOT WANT FROM MY FRIENDS
Possessiveness		
Commitment		
Groups/Cliques		
Authenticity		
Addiction		
Rules		
Risks		
Give and Take		
Decision-Making		
Reliability		
Loyalty		
Other		
Other		
Other		
Other		

(Continued on the next page)

 © 2011 WHOLE PERSON ASSOCIATES, 210 WEST MICHIGAN ST., DULUTH MN 55802-1908 ▪ 800-247-6789

Friendship Situations in Which I Lack Assertiveness

Identify those situations in which you need to be more assertive with your friends. By becoming more aware of those situations in which you are not assertive, you can practice your assertiveness training skills.

For each of the situations listed below, describe how you show a lack of assertiveness.

Situations in which you might lack assertiveness	If you lack assertiveness in this area, why aren't you assertive?
Saying "No" to my friends	*Ex: I am afraid that they will not think I am cool enough to be their friend.*
Asking my friends for favors	
Disagreeing with my friends' opinions	
Using drugs and/or alcohol	
Social situations	
Asking for what I want	
Stating my opinion even if it is different from my friend's opinion	
Asking for help	
Asking for respect	
Asking my friends to listen without judging me	

© 2011 WHOLE PERSON ASSOCIATES, 210 WEST MICHIGAN ST., DULUTH MN 55802-1908 • 800-247-6789

Listening

You wouldn't think that listening is a skill that you possess and that can be used to help improve your friendships. Listening skills are often overlooked in friendships, but can be one of the most critical aspects of communication and understanding between you and your friends. Listening involves an awareness of what your friends are saying to you or asking you to do.

Blocks to Listening

Inadequate listening – It is easy to get distracted from what your friends are saying. This includes things such as thinking too much or thinking about what you need too much. You may be thinking about your own problems or be so eager to help the other person that you are not really listening to what they are saying. Remember too that cultural differences may influence listening styles and require special attention.

Judging – Listening with the intent of judging your friends can hinder your ability to really hear what is being said. You may find that you are judging what your friends are saying as good or bad, right or wrong. You may not be listening to what the person is actually saying. It is important to set your judgments aside when communicating with your friends so that you can hear their point of view on an issue.

Daydreaming – Everyone's attention wanders from time to time. If you find yourself having a difficult time listening to one of your friends, it is probably a sign that you are not interested in the conversation or that you are bored with what your friends are talking about.

Rehearsing – Any time you ask yourself the question "How should I respond to what my friends are saying?" or start rehearsing the way you will answer, you distract yourself from what the other person is saying. As you improve your listening skills, the words will just come naturally. It is best to listen intently to your friends and to focus on the themes and core messages related to their words, and allow your intuition to provide you with a response.

Filtering – Listening to certain parts of the conversation, but not all, can cause trouble. You'll only get a portion of the facts and you will base responses or actions on just part of what you needed to hear.

Distractions – Your attention may be sidetracked by something internal to you (hunger, headache, worry) or external to you (traffic, whispering, other people talking). Concentrating on the conversation and staying in the present will help.

Listening Unrealistically – Listening without questioning the messages being sent from the other person is unrealistic. It is important to be sure you are not being influenced by their popularity, status or promises.

© 2011 WHOLE PERSON ASSOCIATES, 210 WEST MICHIGAN ST., DULUTH MN 55802-1908 ▪ 800-247-6789

Learning to Listen

Listening can be a difficult skill to master because it requires you to hear with your eyes, body and heart, as well as with your ears.

Effective Listening Skills
Focus on what your friends are saying and pay no attention to internal or external happenings.
Listen to the words and tone of voice; notice the body language; feel the sincerity.
Clarify misunderstood points ("What did you mean when you said_____").
Ask questions for more information or clarification ("What video game did you say that was?")

Non-Effective Listening Skills
Focus on your feelings about what your friends are saying.
Listen to the words only and do not pay attention to body language and sincerity.
Feel defensive and rehearse in your mind how to respond.
Judge, label and make assumptions about what is being said.

What do you notice about your listening habits when communicating with your friends?

_____

_____

_____

What do you notice about your friends' listening habits when they communicate?

_____

_____

_____

How can you be a better listener?

_____

_____

_____

In which situations can you be a better listener for your friends?

_____

_____

_____

© 2011 WHOLE PERSON ASSOCIATES, 210 WEST MICHIGAN ST., DULUTH MN 55802-1908 ▪ 800-247-6789

Anger

Remember that anger is a normal emotion. Friends can disagree, but when they do, it does not need to cause angry feelings. Friends are able to express their opinions and needs without hurting each other and making each other angry. Friends are able to resolve their differences and solve problems by working together to find win-win solutions for everyone, while sticking up for what they believe.

Ways to Avoid Arguments

Leave the situation until your angry feelings have passed. Take a walk, call another friend on your cell phone, see a movie or walk your dog until you are ready to discuss the situation more rationally. What types of things could you do the next time you feel an argument escalating?

_____

_____

_____

Use empathy to better understand. Empathy is the ability to put yourself in your friend's shoes and experience what the other person is experiencing.

Think about some situations about which you and your friends argue. List those situations in the left column of the table below. Then in the right column, list some of your insights about the situation if you were to put yourself in that friend's situation.

Things We Argue About (use name code)	**Insights About Why We Argue**
Ex: KLK doesn't always do what he says he'll do.	Ex: KLK has so many commitments at school and home, he can't always follow through.

© 2011 WHOLE PERSON ASSOCIATES, 210 WEST MICHIGAN ST., DULUTH MN 55802-1908 ▪ 800-247-6789

Jumping to Conclusions

False assumptions happen when you or your friends jump to conclusions about each other's thoughts, feelings or actions.

Ways I Jump to Conclusions About My Friends (use name code)
Ex: When I see LML talking with someone I don't know, I think they are gossiping about me.

Ways My Friends Jump to Conclusions About Me
Ex: When MAG texts me and I don't text him back immediately, he thinks I'm angry at him.

© 2011 WHOLE PERSON ASSOCIATES, 210 WEST MICHIGAN ST., DULUTH MN 55802-1908 ▪ 800-247-6789

Communication Skills

Which communication skills do you need most to improve? How will you do that?

_____

_____

_____

_____

_____

_____

_____

_____

How do you feel these communication skills will directly impact your relationships with your friends?

_____

_____

_____

_____

_____

_____

_____

_____

Which communication skills could your friends develop? (Use code name.)

_____

_____

_____

_____

_____

_____

_____

_____

© 2011 WHOLE PERSON ASSOCIATES, 210 WEST MICHIGAN ST., DULUTH MN 55802-1908 ▪ 800-247-6789

Communication Skills Quotations

❑ *Argument is the worst sort of conversation.* ~ **Jonathan Swift**

❑ *The most basic of all human needs is the need to understand and be understood. The best way to understand people is to listen to them.* ~ **Ralph Nichols**

Check one of the quotations above and journal your thoughts.

_____

_____

_____

_____

_____

_____

_____

_____

_____

_____

_____

_____

_____

_____

_____

_____

_____

_____

_____

_____

_____

_____

Ways to Be
a Good Communicator

- Be open, honest and direct.

- Don't interrupt – just listen.

- Send direct, clear verbal messages.

- Pay attention to body language and gestures as well as tone, volume and pitch of voice.

- Communicate assertively.

- Be careful how many times you say, *"Yes, but ..."*

- Focus your full attention on the speaker.

- Be careful when you are communicating electronically.

- Know when to keep a secret and know when NOT to keep a secret if you think someone's at risk.

© 2011 WHOLE PERSON ASSOCIATES, 210 WEST MICHIGAN ST., DULUTH MN 55802-1908 • 800-247-6789

Communication Pitfalls

- Feeling that your friends are always at fault and you are the victim

- Feeling defensive if your friends have an opinion that is different from yours

- Thinking that all people communicate like you do

- Rejecting and devaluing your friends

- Expecting a change in the personality of your friends

- Exchanging unclear and mixed messages with your friends

- Digging up past problems with your friends

- Arguing for the sake of arguing

- Believing everything you are told

© 2011 WHOLE PERSON ASSOCIATES, 210 WEST MICHIGAN ST., DULUTH MN 55802-1908 • 800-247-6789

78

© 2011 WHOLE PERSON ASSOCIATES, 210 WEST MICHIGAN ST., DULUTH MN 55802-1908 ▪ 800-247-6789

SECTION IV:
Friendship Personality Scale

Name_____

Date_____

© 2011 WHOLE PERSON ASSOCIATES, 210 WEST MICHIGAN ST., DULUTH MN 55802-1908 ▪ 800-247-6789

My Personality Scale Directions

Your personality is your usual style of behaving and reacting emotionally. It develops as a result of a combination of traits you inherit and the experiences you have while growing up. Your friends have different types of personalities, some very similar to yours and some quite different. The more you understand your own personality and the personality of your friends, the better your friendships will become because you will accept one another's differences.

The Friendship Personality Scale contains two different assessments. The first is for you to **complete about yourself**. The second is for you to **complete about a friend who is most different from you**. The scales contain a series of words that describe various personality traits that may or may not be applicable. Read each of the words listed on the first scale and circle the words that **describe you**. Then, on the next scale, circle the words that **describe the friend most different from you**. If a word does not apply, do not circle the word, simply move to the next word.

In the example below, the participant circled: genuine, stable, natural, athletic, practical and outdoorsy. Remember, you may circle as many as apply to you, or you may circle none of the items if none of them apply.

I consider MYSELF to be (circle all that apply):

Conforming	Humble	Athletic
Frank	Handy	Persistent
Genuine	Modest	Practical
Hard-headed	Natural	Shy
Honest	Mechanical	Outdoorsy
Stable	Self-reliant	Physical

R TOTAL = _____

This is not a test and there are no right or wrong answers. Take your time responding, but be sure to read each word listed. Circle only the words that apply to you. Your initial response will likely be the most true for you.

(Turn to the next page and begin)

My Personality Scale

I consider MYSELF to be (circle all that apply):

Conforming	Humble	Athletic
Frank	Useful	Persistent
Genuine	Sensible	Practical
Hard-headed	Natural	Shy
Honest	Mechanical	Outdoorsy
Stable	Self-reliant	Physical

R TOTAL = _____

I consider MYSELF to be (circle all that apply):

Analytical	Logical	Reserved
Cautious	Methodical	Resourceful
Complex	Modest	Scholarly
Curious	Pessimistic	Scientific
Intellectual	Precise	Self-controlled
Introverted	Questioning	Systematic

I TOTAL = _____

I consider MYSELF to be (circle all that apply):

Complicated	Imaginative	Creative
Individualistic	Innovative	Intuitive
Emotional	Impulsive	Nonconforming
Expressive	Independent	Open
Idealistic	Artsy	Original
Uncontrolled	Daydreamy	Unstructured

A TOTAL = _____

(Continued on the next page)

 © 2011 WHOLE PERSON ASSOCIATES, 210 WEST MICHIGAN ST., DULUTH MN 55802-1908 ▪ 800-247-6789

(My Personality Scale continued)

I consider MYSELF to be (circle all that apply):

Convincing	Humorous	Sociable
Cooperative	Kind	Friendly
Emotional	Patient	Tactful
Generous	Responsible	Understanding
Helpful	Caring	Warm
Humanistic	People-oriented	Cheerful

S TOTAL = _____

I consider MYSELF to be (circle all that apply):

Inquisitive	Domineering	Optimistic
Adventurous	Energetic	Assertive
Bold	Extroverted	Popular
Ambitious	Impulsive	Self-confident
Attention-getting	Persuasive	Sociable
Aggressive	Charismatic	Goal-driven

E TOTAL = _____

I consider MYSELF to be (circle all that apply):

Conforming	Inhibited	Persistent
Conscientious	Self-Disciplined	Practical
Careful	Orderly	Thrifty
Efficient	Unimaginative	Reserved
Structured	Precise	Organized
Scheduled	Dependable	Self-controlled

T TOTAL = _____

(Go to the Scoring Directions on the next page)

My Personality Scale Scoring

Count the total number of items you circled for each section. Put that number on the line marked TOTAL at the bottom of each of section and then transfer your totals to the spaces below:

_____	=	R	(Realistic)
_____	=	I	(Investigative)
_____	=	A	(Artistic)
_____	=	S	(Social)
_____	=	E	(Enterprising)
_____	=	T	(Traditional)

Profile Interpretation

INDIVIDUAL SCALE SCORE	RESULT	INDICATIONS
Scores from 0 to 5	Low	You probably do not possess many of the characteristics of this personality type.
Scores from 6 to 12	Moderate	You probably possess some of the characteristics of this personality type.
Scores from 13 to 18	High	You probably possess many of the characteristics of this personality type.

Generally the higher your score, the more characteristics you share with others of that personality type. Identify the scale on which you scored the highest. This is your primary personality type. Read about your personality type(s) as well as all of the other types in the descriptions that follow. You and your friends are probably a combination of personalities, depending on your different roles. Complete the questions at the bottom of the descriptions.

© 2011 WHOLE PERSON ASSOCIATES, 210 WEST MICHIGAN ST., DULUTH MN 55802-1908 ▪ 800-247-6789

Scale Description for a Realistic Personality

People scoring high on the Realistic Scale tend to be realistic about themselves and their friendships. They tend to be reliable friends. When they say they will do something, they will honor their commitments. They focus on the day-to-day business of living their lives and enjoy doing favors for their friends and being supportive. They enjoy working outside on activities or activities with machines rather than with people. They usually are not too interested in indoor social activities, and would much rather be outdoors.

Realistic personalities enjoy trying to make things grow and prosper. They are primarily interested in practical, earthy matters, granting them the ability to develop the things they feel are most worthy. They tend to have a no-nonsense approach to life and to their friendships. They tend to "say it like it is."

Realistic personalities are not always interested in getting rich or famous. They enjoy accomplishing things, but enjoy the process of simply getting things done. They are rarely interested in generating ideas, being innovative, or in trying to understand complex formulas. Rather they enjoy things that are easy to experience and that they can feel, taste, hear, and smell.

Realistic personalities seek stability and security in their friendships. They are reliable, stubborn, down-to-earth, independent and true to their word.

In what ways does this describe you?

_____

_____

_____

_____

_____

_____

In what ways does this description not fit you?

_____

_____

_____

_____

_____

_____

© 2011 WHOLE PERSON ASSOCIATES, 210 WEST MICHIGAN ST., DULUTH MN 55802-1908 ▪ 800-247-6789

Scale Description
for an Investigative Personality

People scoring high on the Investigative Scale enjoy activities in which they can be stimulated intellectually. They are bright and curious, and tend to be lifelong students. They are very inquisitive and driven by the desire to research and learn new things and search for answers to life's mysteries. They are often perceived as being scholarly, analytic, critical, introspective and methodical.

Investigative personalities tend to live in the world of ideas and concepts and sometimes lose sight of the importance of friendships. They enjoy talking about their ideas with others, but they can find it difficult to become fully engaged with other people. This communication problem can cause arguments in some friendships. They generally enjoy leisure activities like reading books and going to concerts, reading about and using new technology, school and lectures.

Investigative personalities are most comfortable thinking rather than feeling or acting. They are always searching for information that they can use to their advantage. They do not get bogged down in details but usually look at the big picture. For the Investigative personality, understanding why people do things in life is just as much fun as living it.

Investigative personalities tend to be quiet and thoughtful, and enjoy spending a lot of time alone. This can cause conflict in some relationships when friends (who have different personality types) find it hard to understand why Investigative personality types need time by themselves to recharge their batteries.

In what ways does this describe you?

_____

_____

_____

_____

_____

In what ways does this description not fit you?

_____

_____

_____

_____

_____

© 2011 WHOLE PERSON ASSOCIATES, 210 WEST MICHIGAN ST., DULUTH MN 55802-1908 ▪ 800-247-6789

Scale Description for an Artistic Personality

People scoring high on the Artistic Scale tend to see life and friendships from a holistic point of view so that they are always looking at the big picture. They avoid highly structured situations in which they cannot be spontaneous. They are creative and love to work on creative projects.

Artistic personalities are able to create beautiful pictures in their mind and then make those pictures a reality through such activities as writing, singing, drawing, sculpting and acting. They always look for new interests and often have difficulty staying with tasks to completion, making them long on vision and a little short on action.

Artistic personalities want to make the world a better and different place through their creative accomplishments. This is expressed through activities such as: music, dance, acting, theater, writing, entertaining, and art in any form. Nearly everything they do is a search for a way to express their uniqueness and individuality. They have a very highly developed artistic sense and often do not care if other people think they are different or unique.

Artistic personalities tend to be shy and introverted, and thus are not usually comfortable in large groups of people, even with friends. They find that many adults in their life try to restrict their individuality and creativity. They tend to create alone, working tirelessly to see their accomplishments come alive.

In what ways does this describe you?

_____

_____

_____

_____

_____

_____

In what ways does this description not fit you?

_____

_____

_____

_____

_____

_____

Scale Description for a Social Personality

People who score high on the Social Scale love to be with other people and are good at picking up on their friends' moods and feelings. They like to help and support their friends when a problem arises because they have a strong concern for the welfare of others. They enjoy giving friends their time and understanding. They are compassionate and nurturing.

Social personalities are interested in and working in their community in jobs like counseling, teaching or some type of helping position. They prefer to deal with people rather than with ideas or things. They value the supportive and emotional rewards they receive from their friends. They are willing and eager to learn about themselves and work on improving their relationships with their friends.

Social personalities often invest a lot of effort, emotion, and enthusiasm in their friendships, but sometimes more than their friends need or want. While their life and their friendships tend to be practical in nature, they are often helping and social in nature. Other people often view them as being naïve or unrealistic.

Social personalities are determined to stick to their principles, and they strive to find friends who have similar values. They are very thoughtful and emotional, but are equally capable of taking quick and decisive action when their friends are in need. They value friends who are honest and authentic.

In what ways does this describe you?

_____

_____

_____

_____

_____

_____

In what ways does this description not fit you?

_____

_____

_____

_____

_____

_____

© 2011 WHOLE PERSON ASSOCIATES, 210 WEST MICHIGAN ST., DULUTH MN 55802-1908 ▪ 800-247-6789

Scale Description for an Enterprising Personality

People who score high on the Enterprising Scale like to take the lead and like to be assertive in their friendship. They like to have the power and status that comes with being in charge. They strive to be the best at what they do and the first to do it. They are confident and determined and have natural leadership abilities; in many cases they just prefer to get things done themselves. They are also highly persuasive and charismatic in their friendships.

Enterprising personalities prefer to be in charge. They make decisions quickly whether others like it or not. They understand power and the impact that it can have on their life and the lives of their friends. They also have a gift for bringing out the strengths of their friends. They tend to understand and appreciate the power of money, and strive to attain it, control it, and put it to good use.

Enterprising personalities are usually eager to take on new projects and challenges. Their confidence and determination makes "all things possible," and allows them to get the support of other people around them. They are always looking for ways that their friends can be better off. Perhaps more than any other personality, they envision and plan for success.

In what ways does this describe you?

_____

_____

_____

_____

_____

_____

In what ways does this description not fit you?

_____

_____

_____

_____

_____

_____

Scale Description
for a Traditional Personality

People who score high on the Traditional Scale tend to be neat, organized, and always under control in their friendships. They are able to concentrate on the task at hand and are excellent with details. They are organized to the point of sometimes being inflexible and stubborn, and they prefer to follow strict guidelines. They often get stuck on a concept, idea or plan, and have a hard time breaking habits.

Traditional personalities often prefer activities that involve data and information rather than people or ideas. They pay great attention to details and are often counted on for their dependability and reliability in a relationship. They are practical, hardworking, and traditional, and they enjoy solving problems provided there is a set procedure to follow. They make excellent day-to-day managers, though they prefer to run and organize their friendships from behind the scenes.

Traditional personalities truly value success and happiness in a relationship and will do everything in their power to ensure that success. They are conscientious, stable, thorough, conservative, enjoy life when everything runs according to their plans. Their planning can become obsessive and can cause problems in some friendships.

In what ways does this describe you?

_____

_____

_____

_____

_____

In what ways does this description not fit you?

_____

_____

_____

_____

_____

_____

© 2011 WHOLE PERSON ASSOCIATES, 210 WEST MICHIGAN ST., DULUTH MN 55802-1908 ▪ 800-247-6789

How I View the Friend Who Is Most Different from Me Scale

It might be fun now to retake the assessment, but this time, circle descriptors based on how you see the personality of one of your friends who is most different from you. Write your friend's code name: _____. Now, circle the words that follow based on how you view this friend's personality:

I consider my FRIEND to be (circle all that apply):

Conforming	Humble	Athletic
Frank	Useful	Persistent
Genuine	Sensible	Practical
Hard-headed	Natural	Shy
Honest	Mechanical	Outdoorsy
Stable	Self-reliant	Physical
		R TOTAL = _____

Analytical	Logical	Reserved
Cautious	Methodical	Resourceful
Complex	Modest	Scholarly
Curious	Pessimistic	Scientific
Intellectual	Precise	Self-controlled
Introverted	Questioning	Systematic
		I TOTAL = _____

Complicated	Imaginative	Creative
Individualistic	Innovative	Intuitive
Emotional	Impulsive	Nonconforming
Expressive	Independent	Open
Idealistic	Artsy	Original
Uncontrolled	Daydreamy	Unstructured
		A TOTAL = _____

(Continued on the next page)

How I View the Friend Who Is
Most Different from Me Scale *(Continued)*

I consider my FRIEND to be (circle all that apply):

Convincing	Humorous	Sociable
Cooperative	Kind	Friendly
Emotional	Patient	Tactful
Generous	Responsible	Understanding
Helpful	Caring	Warm
Humanistic	People-oriented	Cheerful

S TOTAL = _____

Inquisitive	Domineering	Optimistic
Adventurous	Energetic	Assertive
Bold	Extroverted	Popular
Ambitious	Impulsive	Self-confident
Attention-getting	Persuasive	Sociable
Aggressive	Charismatic	Goal-driven

E TOTAL = _____

Conforming	Inhibited	Persistent
Conscientious	Self-Disciplined	Practical
Careful	Orderly	Thrifty
Efficient	Unimaginative	Reserved
Structured	Precise	Organized
Scheduled	Dependable	Self-controlled

T TOTAL = _____

© 2011 WHOLE PERSON ASSOCIATES, 210 WEST MICHIGAN ST., DULUTH MN 55802-1908 ▪ 800-247-6789

How I View the Friend Who Is Most Different from Me Scale Scoring

Count the total number of items you circled for each section. Put that number on the line marked TOTAL at the bottom of each of section and then transfer your totals to the spaces below:

_____ = R (Realistic)

_____ = I (Investigative)

_____ = A (Artistic)

_____ = S (Social)

_____ = E (Enterprising)

_____ = T (Traditional)

Profile Interpretation

INDIVIDUAL SCALE SCORE	RESULT	INDICATIONS
Scores from 0 to 5	Low	Your friend does not possess many of the characteristics of this personality type.
Scores from 6 to 12	Moderate	Your friend probably possesses some of the characteristics of this personality type.
Scores from 13 to 18	High	Your friend probably possesses many of the characteristics of this personality type.

Comparing Personalities

You can now compare your personality with that of your friend. To do so, list your scores for the six scales and those scores for your friend. Then compare and contrast the results.

Myself	Personality Scales	My Friend
	R (Realistic)	
	I (Investigative)	
	A (Artistic)	
	S (Social)	
	E (Enterprising)	
	T (Traditional)	

How were the scores for you and your friend on the assessments similar?

_____

_____

_____

_____

How were the scores for you and your friend on the assessments different?

_____

_____

_____

_____

(Continued on the next page)

© 2011 WHOLE PERSON ASSOCIATES, 210 WEST MICHIGAN ST., DULUTH MN 55802-1908 ▪ 800-247-6789

Comparing Personalities *(Continued)*

What does this say about your friendship?

_____

_____

_____

_____

What have you learned about your friend's personality?

_____

_____

_____

_____

How do the similarities (if any) enhance your friendship?

_____

_____

_____

_____

_____

How do the differences detract from your friendship?

_____

_____

_____

_____

How do the differences enhance your friendship?

_____

_____

_____

_____

(Continued on the next page)

© 2011 WHOLE PERSON ASSOCIATES, 210 WEST MICHIGAN ST., DULUTH MN 55802-1908 ▪ 800-247-6789

Comparing Personalities *(Continued)*

In what ways do you wish this friend would change?

_____

_____

_____

_____

In what ways do you wish this friend would stay the same?

_____

_____

_____

_____

In what ways do you try and change your true personality to accommodate your friends?

_____

_____

_____

_____

What aspects of your personality would you like to change?

_____

_____

_____

_____

_____

_____

_____

_____

© 2011 WHOLE PERSON ASSOCIATES, 210 WEST MICHIGAN ST., DULUTH MN 55802-1908 ▪ 800-247-6789

Diversity

Based on what you have learned about yourself and your friends, choose 3 friends, write their code name with 3 positive qualities of each.

Friend #1: Code Name _____

    1) _____

    2) _____

    3) _____

Friend #2: Code Name _____

    1) _____

    2) _____

    3) _____

Friend #3: Code Name _____

    1) _____

    2) _____

    3) _____

Now choose 3 friends (other friends or the same) and their negative characteristics of each.

Friend #1: Code Name _____

    1) _____

    2) _____

    3) _____

Friend #2: Code Name _____

    1) _____

    2) _____

    3) _____

Friend #3: Code Name _____

    1) _____

    2) _____

    3) _____

© 2011 WHOLE PERSON ASSOCIATES, 210 WEST MICHIGAN ST., DULUTH MN 55802-1908 ▪ 800-247-6789

About Personalities

Things to remember about your personality and the personalities of your friends . . .

- You probably cannot change your basic personality type, but you can change behaviors associated with your basic type.

- All types have unique sets of strengths and weaknesses.

- No personality type is better than any other personality type.

- All of the information you read about your type may not apply to you all of the time.

- People with similar personality types tend to be motivated in the same ways, view the world in a similar manner, and engage in similar activities.

- Factors such as where you were born and raised, your family's socio-economic status, and the cultural values you inherit can influence the intensity of your personality type.

- Friends do not necessarily need to have similar personality types to have great relationships.

Think about this quotation and either discuss or journal your thoughts.

Watch your thoughts, for they become words.

Watch your words, for they become actions.

Watch your actions for they become habits.

Watch your habits, for they become character.

Watch your character, for it becomes your destiny.

© 2011 WHOLE PERSON ASSOCIATES, 210 WEST MICHIGAN ST., DULUTH MN 55802-1908 • 800-247-6789

Personality and Relationships

Your personality affects your friendships in a variety of ways including . . .

- How you make decisions

- How you interact with your friends

- Why you are drawn to certain hobbies and social activities

- How you interact with other people

- The amount of time you want to spend with your friends

- How you value differences in your friends

- How you solve problems and resolve conflicts with your friends

- How seriously you take your commitments

- How you value diversity

© 2011 WHOLE PERSON ASSOCIATES, 210 WEST MICHIGAN ST., DULUTH MN 55802-1908 ▪ 800-247-6789

SECTION V:
Peer Pressure Scale

Name_____

Date_____

© 2011 WHOLE PERSON ASSOCIATES, 210 WEST MICHIGAN ST., DULUTH MN 55802-1908 ▪ 800-247-6789

Peer Pressure Scale Directions

You probably deal with peer pressure everyday and in a variety of ways. Peer pressure can be positive or negative. It happens in school, at work, at the local mall, and anywhere else you hang out with your friends. You are not alone; all people experience peer pressure or have experienced it in the past. The Peer Pressure Scale can help you to identify the ways in which you feel pressured by your friends to do things you may or may not want to do.

This section includes two scales:

- Positive Peer Pressure
- Negative Peer Pressure

Each scale contains 30 statements. On both scales, read each of the statements and circle YES if the statement describes you and circle NO if the statement does not describe you. You will be asked to identify the friend by his/her code name.

In the following examples, the circled YES indicates that both statements are **True** for the person completing the scale.

Example – Positive Peer Pressure Scale:

This friend sometimes encourages me to . . .

care about other people NO

Example – Negative Peer Pressure Scale:

My friend sometimes pressures me to . . .

go to parties that I am not comfortable going to NO

This is not a test and there are no right or wrong answers. Do not spend too much time thinking about your answers. Your initial response will likely be the most true for you. Be sure to respond to every statement.

(Turn to the next page and begin)

© 2011 WHOLE PERSON ASSOCIATES, 210 WEST MICHIGAN ST., DULUTH MN 55802-1908 ▪ 800-247-6789

Positive Peer Pressure Scale

The friend I will be referring to is _____ (code name)

This friend sometimes encourages me to . . .

care about other people	YES	NO
volunteer my time	YES	NO
try to make the world a better place	YES	NO
help to make my community better	YES	NO
get involved in community affairs	YES	NO

C TOTAL _____

This friend sometimes encourages me to . . .

work on getting good grades	YES	NO
think about how school will help me in the future	YES	NO
complete assignments on time	YES	NO
stay in school even if I don't want to	YES	NO
continue my education after I graduate	YES	NO

S TOTAL _____

This friend sometimes encourages me to . . .

respect other people	YES	NO
enjoy the differences in my friends	YES	NO
give people the benefit of the doubt	YES	NO
respect people older than I	YES	NO
work cooperatively as a team	YES	NO

R TOTAL _____

(Continued on the next page)

© 2011 WHOLE PERSON ASSOCIATES, 210 WEST MICHIGAN ST., DULUTH MN 55802-1908 ▪ 800-247-6789

(Positive Peer Pressure Scale continued)

This friend sometimes encourages me to . . .

eat and drink healthy foods and beverages	YES	NO
exercise and maintain physical fitness	YES	NO
participate in some sort of sports	YES	NO
engage in healthy behaviors	YES	NO
find ways to reduce my stress	YES	NO

H TOTAL _____

This friend sometimes encourages me to . . .

be optimistic	YES	NO
enjoy life and have healthy fun	YES	NO
live in the present moment	YES	NO
make decisions logically	YES	NO
think for myself	YES	NO

T TOTAL _____

This friend sometimes encourages me to . . .

reach my full potential	YES	NO
strive to do my best	YES	NO
do well in everything I do	YES	NO
be true to myself	YES	NO
use all of my skills and unique talents	YES	NO

SU TOTAL _____

(Go to the Scoring Directions on the next page)

Positive Peer Pressure Scale
Scoring Directions

Some friends will encourage and pressure you in a positive way. For each of the six sections on the previous pages, count the number of YES answers you circled. Put that total on the line marked TOTAL at the end of each section.

Transfer your totals to the spaces below:

C – COMMUNITY   TOTAL = _____

S – SCHOOL   TOTAL = _____

R – RESPECT   TOTAL = _____

H – HEALTH   TOTAL = _____

T – THINKING   TOTAL = _____

SU – SUPPORT   TOTAL = _____

ADD YOUR OVERALL TOTAL = _____

Profile Interpretation

INDIVIDUAL SCALE SCORES	TOTAL SCORE ALL SIX SCALES	RESULT	INDICATIONS
Scores from 4 to 5	Scores from 21 to 30	High	If you score high on any individual scale or all scales, your friends are **definitely** encouraging you to become a better person.
Scores from 2 to 3	Scores from 10 to 20	Moderate	If you score moderate on any individual scale or all scales, your friends are **mildly** encouraging you to become a better person.
Scores from 0 to 1	Scores from 0 to 9	Low	If you score low on any or all scales, your friends are **not** encouraging you to become a better person.

For scales which you scored in the **Moderate** or **High** range, find the descriptions on the pages that follow. Then, read the description and complete the exercises that are included. No matter how you scored, low, moderate or high, you will benefit from these exercises.

© 2011 WHOLE PERSON ASSOCIATES, 210 WEST MICHIGAN ST., DULUTH MN 55802-1908 • 800-247-6789

Community

Note a time when a friend encouraged you to be involved positively in your community.

Code name _____

_____

_____

How did you respond?

_____

_____

What was the outcome?

_____

_____

What have you learned?

_____

_____

School

List a time when a friend encouraged you to do well in school.

Code name _____

_____

_____

How did you respond?

_____

_____

What was the outcome?

_____

_____

What have you learned?

_____

_____

© 2011 WHOLE PERSON ASSOCIATES, 210 WEST MICHIGAN ST., DULUTH MN 55802-1908 ▪ 800-247-6789

Respect

List a time when a friend encouraged you to be respectful to someone else or yourself.

Code name _____

_____

_____

How did you respond?

_____

_____

What was the outcome?

_____

_____

What have you learned?

_____

_____

Health

List a time when a friend encouraged you live a healthier lifestyle.

Code name _____

_____

_____

How did you respond?

_____

_____

What was the outcome?

_____

_____

What have you learned?

_____

_____

© 2011 WHOLE PERSON ASSOCIATES, 210 WEST MICHIGAN ST., DULUTH MN 55802-1908 ▪ 800-247-6789

Positive Thinking

List a time when a friend encouraged you to be a creative and positive thinker.

Code name _____

_____

_____

How did you respond?

_____

_____

What was the outcome?

_____

_____

What have you learned?

_____

_____

Support

List a time when a friend encouraged and supported you in a positive way.

Code name _____

_____

_____

How did you respond?

_____

_____

What was the outcome?

_____

_____

What have you learned?

_____

_____

© 2011 WHOLE PERSON ASSOCIATES, 210 WEST MICHIGAN ST., DULUTH MN 55802-1908 ▪ 800-247-6789

Negative Peer Pressure Scale

The friend I will be referring to is _____ (code name)

This friend sometimes pressures me to . . .

go to parties that I am not comfortable going to	YES	NO
host parties in my house when my family is not home	YES	NO
drink alcohol	YES	NO
explore drugs	YES	NO
smoke	YES	NO

S TOTAL _____

This friend sometimes pressures me to . . .

shoplift	YES	NO
do things that are against the law	YES	NO
vandalize	YES	NO
hurt animals or people	YES	NO
engage in illegal activities	YES	NO

C TOTAL _____

This friend sometimes pressures me to . . .

show off what I have	YES	NO
spend money for things I cannot afford	YES	NO
make fun of people who have less than I	YES	NO
talk, do things and/or act in ways I usually wouldn't do	YES	NO
wear the latest styles even if I don't care about fads or trends	YES	NO

L TOTAL _____

(Continued on the next page)

 © 2011 WHOLE PERSON ASSOCIATES, 210 WEST MICHIGAN ST., DULUTH MN 55802-1908 ▪ 800-247-6789

(Negative Peer Pressure Scale continued)

This friend sometimes pressures me to . . .

cut classes	YES	NO
drop out of school	YES	NO
go out and not bother to do my chores or homework	YES	NO
cheat on tests	YES	NO
drop out of organized extracurricular activities	YES	NO

SC TOTAL _____

This friend sometimes pressures me to . . .

tease other people	YES	NO
fight with other people	YES	NO
bully other people	YES	NO
threaten other people	YES	NO
promote hatred of people who are different	YES	NO

B TOTAL _____

This friend sometimes pressures me to . . .

be disrespectful to others	YES	NO
be intimate before I want to	YES	NO
lie to the adults in my life	YES	NO
sneak out of the house	YES	NO
brush-off other people	YES	NO

A TOTAL _____

(Go to the Scoring Directions on the next page)

© 2011 WHOLE PERSON ASSOCIATES, 210 WEST MICHIGAN ST., DULUTH MN 55802-1908 • 800-247-6789

Negative Peer Pressure Scale
Scoring Directions

People feel pressured to do things they would not ordinarily do because they want to fit in and be popular; they don't want to be labeled as an outcast or loser. For each of the six sections on the previous pages, count the number of YES answers you circled. Put that total on the line marked TOTAL at the end of each section.

Transfer your totals to the spaces below:

S - SUBSTANCES   TOTAL = _____

C – CRIMINAL BEHAVIOR   TOTAL = _____

L - LIFESTYLE   TOTAL = _____

SC - SCHOOL   TOTAL = _____

B - BULLYING   TOTAL = _____

A - ATTITUDE   TOTAL = _____

_____

ADD YOUR OVERALL TOTAL = _____

Profile Interpretation

INDIVIDUAL SCALE SCORES	TOTAL SCORE ALL SIX SCALES	RESULT	INDICATIONS
Scores from 4 to 5	Scores from 21 to 30	High	If you score high on any or all scales, your friends are **pressuring** you to do things you do not want to do.
Scores from 2 to 3	Scores from 10 to 20	Moderate	If you score moderate on any or all scales, your friends are applying **some pressure** for you to do things you do not want to do.
Scores from 0 to 1	Scores from 0 to 9	Low	If you score low on any or all scales, your friends are **not pressuring** you to do things you do not want to do.

For scales which you scored in the **Moderate** or **High** range, find the descriptions on the pages that follow. Then, read the description and complete the exercises that are included. No matter how you scored, low, moderate or high, you will benefit from these exercises.

© 2011 WHOLE PERSON ASSOCIATES, 210 WEST MICHIGAN ST., DULUTH MN 55802-1908 ▪ 800-247-6789

Substances

List a time when a friend pressured you into taking a risk by experimenting with, or using, substances. If you have experienced this type of situation, respond below.

Code name _____

_____

_____

Why did you take that risk?

_____

What was the outcome of the risk?

_____

How did you feel about yourself?

_____

What have you learned?

_____

_____

Criminal Behavior

List a time when a friend pressured you into taking a risk engaging in criminal behavior. If you have experienced this type of situation, respond below.

Code name _____

_____

_____

Why did you take that risk?

_____

What was the outcome of the risk?

_____

How did you feel about yourself?

_____

What have you learned?

_____

_____

Lifestyle

List a time when a friend pressured you into taking a risk by exhibiting similar lifestyle behaviors as the people in their clique. If you have experienced this type of situation, respond below.

Code name _____

_____

_____

Why did you take that risk?

_____

What was the outcome of the risk?

_____

How did you feel about yourself?

_____

What have you learned?

_____

_____

School

List a time when a friend pressured you into taking a risk by getting into trouble at school. If you have experienced this type of situation, respond below.

Code name _____

_____

_____

Why did you take that risk?

_____

What was the outcome of the risk?

_____

How did you feel about yourself?

_____

What have you learned?

_____

_____

© 2011 WHOLE PERSON ASSOCIATES, 210 WEST MICHIGAN ST., DULUTH MN 55802-1908 ▪ 800-247-6789

Bullying

List a time when a friend pressured you into taking a risk by bullying others. If you have experienced this type of situation, respond below.

Code name _____

_____

_____

Why did you take that risk?

_____

What was the outcome of the risk?

_____

How did you feel about yourself?

_____

What have you learned?

_____

_____

Attitude

List a time when a friend pressured you into altering your normal attitude. If you have experienced this type of situation, respond below.

Code name _____

_____

_____

Why did you take that risk?

_____

What was the outcome of the risk?

_____

How did you feel about yourself?

_____

What have you learned?

_____

_____

Negative Peer Pressure

Peer pressure is defined as the pressure you feel from your peers to do things that you would normally not do. Regardless of how old you are, there will always be pressure to conform to certain friendship norms, and these pressures could possibly put you at risk or make you compromise your morals and values. Think about some of the reasons that you give in to peer pressure from your friends. In the table that follows, think about some of the traits listed that can put you at higher risk for giving in to peer pressure. Then list how these risk factors make you vulnerable to peer pressure.

List a specific time you gave into peer pressure: _____

_____

Risk Factors	How this leads (or could have lead) to problems
Bad feelings about yourself	
Little or no self-confidence	
Few other friendships	
Loneliness	
Wanting and/or needing to be liked and accepted	
Isolation from family and other friends	
Poor academic performance	
Fear of your friends' reactions to you	

What did you learn about yourself from this exercise?

_____

_____

What changes will you make (if any) in your relationship with your friends?

_____

_____

© 2011 WHOLE PERSON ASSOCIATES, 210 WEST MICHIGAN ST., DULUTH MN 55802-1908 • 800-247-6789

From Negative to Positive

Knowing how to handle negative peer pressure is an important friendship skill to learn. It is tough to say NO to peer pressure, but you can do it! You can do several things to help you say NO when the time comes.

In the space that follows:

1) Develop and rehearse a mental script that you can use when you need to deal with an uncomfortable situation in which you are feeling pressured to do something you do not want to do. In the table that follows, develop a script for each of the peer pressure areas in your friendships.

Peer Pressure Areas	My Scripts
Substances	Ex."No thanks, I have seen what cigarettes can do. I have known of people who have died from lung cancer and I don't want that to happen to me."
Substances	
Criminal Behavior	
Lifestyle	
School	
Bullying	
Attitude	

(Continued on the next page)

From Negative to Positive *(Continued)*

2) Be more comfortable in saying NO. The secret is to be assertive and stand up for your right to choose to not engage in the behavior without putting the other person down.

3) You may need to choose other friends who share the same interests and values as you. Think about other people you might like to become friends with. List one in each of the left column blocks, and in the right column blocks, note how each one is are like you.

Potential Friend (code name)	**Why they are like me**

(Continued on the next page)

© 2011 WHOLE PERSON ASSOCIATES, 210 WEST MICHIGAN ST., DULUTH MN 55802-1908 ▪ 800-247-6789

From Negative to Positive *(Continued)*

4) Join clubs or organizations whose members have similar interests as you.

Some of these clubs and organizations . . .

_____

_____

_____

_____

5) What opinions and fears can you discuss with your close adults to get their advice and support?

_____

_____

_____

_____

6) Think of an adult who supports you. What is one issue in which you would benefit by talking with that person?

_____

_____

_____

_____

7) Write a script of how you can begin that conversation.

_____

_____

_____

_____

8) Know what your values and morals are, and then take a stand when you need to. Review your values (doing well in school, being respectful, accepting differences, being honest, etc.).

What are your values?

_____

_____

_____

_____

Peer Pressure

Journal about an example of positive peer pressure you have experienced or witnessed recently. *(Ex. I was about to try a cigarette for the first time and a friend said to me, "Do you really want to do that?")*

_____

_____

_____

_____

_____

_____

_____

_____

_____

_____

Journal about an example of negative peer pressure you have experienced or witnessed recently. *(Ex. I saw a friend agree to have a party when his family would be out of town so that he would be accepted into a popular group.)*

_____

_____

_____

_____

_____

_____

_____

_____

_____

© 2011 WHOLE PERSON ASSOCIATES, 210 WEST MICHIGAN ST., DULUTH MN 55802-1908 ▪ 800-247-6789

Conscience Quotations

Conscience is a person's compass. ~ **Vincent Van Gogh**

Follow your conscience and not the crowd. ~ **Anonymous**

Conscience is the impulse to do right because it is right, regardless of personal ends.
~ **Margaret C. Graham**

Conscience is that still, small voice that is sometimes too loud for comfort. ~ **Bert Murray**

Conscience is what hurts when everything else feels so good. ~ **Anonymous**

Journal your thoughts about any of the above quotations and how each applies to you.

_____

_____

_____

_____

_____

_____

_____

_____

_____

_____

_____

_____

_____

_____

_____

_____

_____

_____

_____

_____

_____

_____

Positive Peer Pressure

Peers can influence each other in positive ways:

- Accepting people different from you
- Acting with respect to family and all adults
- Becoming responsible
- Belonging to school, community or house of worship clubs
- Doing volunteer work
- Eating and drinking healthy food and beverages
- Exercising
- Finding a job
- Following rules
- Helping others
- Joining a school service group
- Meeting new people
- Participating in sports
- Planning on further education
- Refusing to drink and drive
- Rejecting the idea of compromising values
- Respecting property of others
- Studying to earn good grades
- Trying something new that would be beneficial

© 2011 WHOLE PERSON ASSOCIATES, 210 WEST MICHIGAN ST., DULUTH MN 55802-1908 ▪ 800-247-6789

Negative Peer Pressure

Peers can influence each other in negative ways:

- Breaking laws
- Bullying others
- Cheating
- Cutting class
- Developing eating habits that lead to disorders
- Displaying a disrespectful attitude towards others
- Doing things you KNOW you shouldn't do
- Drinking when you are not ready
- Dropping out of school
- Enjoying inappropriate humor: victim, racial, ethnic, put-down and gender jokes, pranks and exploitive humor
- Harassing
- Having an intimate relationship when you're not ready
- Joining a questionable group or gang
- Lying to friends, parents, family, teachers and adults
- Seeking porn
- Showing prejudices
- Smoking
- Stealing
- Using obscene gestures or language
- Vandalizing public or private property

© 2011 WHOLE PERSON ASSOCIATES, 210 WEST MICHIGAN ST., DULUTH MN 55802-1908 ▪ 800-247-6789